GAG ORDER

GAG ORDER

AMERICA'S CLANDESTINE WAR ON DIVERSITY

Timothy Wall

Library of Congress Control Number: 2021911439
ISBN: Hardcover   978-1-6641-7910-3
             Softcover   978-1-6641-7909-7
             eBook   978-1-6641-7908-0

Print information available on the last page.

Rev. date: 06/07/2021

To order additional copies of this book, contact:
Xlibris
844-714-8691
www.Xlibris.com
Orders@Xlibris.com
815160

CONTENTS

Intro: This is the viewpoint of one man's perspective of being run over in America and Internationally by Friends Family Strangers Good people, Bad people, thugs, Rouge individuals, Hackers, Local law enforcement, State Law enforcement, Multiple States, And State Department. For being a happy Go Lucky sexually open, interesting, caring person.

Ok I admit I'm a little dodgy, quirky, comes with the territory of being highly creative. But if you can't tell if someone is saving people or killing them after a lifetime, let alone if someone is violent or not, then laws need to change.

Sexually open people may need to be a protected group. Some may not give a crap about kids, some may actually look to protect kids. Some may be violent and others may not. Most people don't seem to understand sexually open.

At the time I am writing this I am using an old Pc and parts I salvaged from a construction job a year ago. I had to find a hack in to the system to write this due to security settings. I am homeless, run into bankruptcy, Disabled, also recovering from possibly another attempted poisoning just a few days ago. Not to mention countless blocks I can't go into to get this information out and published

The bias is unbelievable. Not unlike Planet of the Apes.

It's my understanding that people who drink may have a higher IQ than those that don't. [Source] The New Republic; Do smart people drink more? By Alice Robb. December 3rd 2013. I also think the same is true for sexually open, diverse, or navigating people.

I think half the people in the country are financially challenged, the other half are millionaires?

I would also say that half the country is sexually diverse navigating or open and the other half are in denial.

Blocking my financial endeavors for nearly two decades until homeless is not a test, it's an execution. National security? I think people in power can do a hell of a lot better. It looks more like a group of older white conservative men afraid to have a conversation about sex.

And another group of older white men attacking the same group. Blocking them till homeless, then manipulating the legal system and provoking violence. One swing inside or out and never seen again.

This is the biggest crock of shit I have ever seen. It's too easy to get in front of the violence and stop it from all sides. People are getting slaughtered. This is a racist war and a government failure.

Set up a conscience dialogue.

Chapter 1

Tip of the spear

Tip of the spear is an internal terrorist group within the US. They create violence, and destroy families. They probably are associated with local law enforcement due to the seamless intel they contain.

The individuals most likely branch outward into other family members, non-law enforcement, and even friends and other random members, groups, criminals and other rogue individuals.

They use hypnosis every day for years on my kid through modern technology to get to me. They imply it does not harm anyone. Nothing could be farther from the truth. This isn't about kids its abought massaging their own ego.

They live, work and go to church general USA They spread

hate and sell violence to as many people they can. This is primarily a white middle class group that looks like they have grown up believing everything on TV. Trapped somewhere between not having tasted wealth or poverty. Perhaps to fill some missing personal self-worth. This is coupled with a dementia backed by ego. Very bias, racist, and extremely dangerous.

This symbol Represents an internal Terrorist Group in the United States.

2021

Chapter 2

Kensho

"Normal competitive bias has replaced perception of threat." T.J.W.

My personal experience is that Kensho does not follow people's logic at least 65% of the time. And that is ongoing. That is to say when I get my feedback from my surroundings it looks like most of the time people have no idea of what is important to someone under life death fear.

Creating life death fear and then setting someone up in different situations. I may have mentioned this in social media already. Risk analysis shifts under threat of death opening up unusual activity and or risky action to avoid further conflict or death. Maintaining status quo may be riskier to life. Most people have no idea of the violent platform that is being created.

Kensho may not work like people want it to, is as a tool. Because the initial impact is so violent to get people to run. If they are smart they will run anyway. They will kill anyway even if they don't know why this is going on.

Every phase after that may be considered life death violence regardless of how seemingly insignificant. Meanwhile every day is destroying the human cells, organs, and system till death or near death. With no public trial in sight.

Association of life death violence may be directed seemingly at will to any existing path or association. For example, kids, sex, work, laptop computers, America, and people and family.

Basically Kensho is this Tip of the spear group executing people through violence, or setting up people to incarcerate them, through financial lack of payment or violence, or blocking legal information and using it against them. Or anyway they can provoke you. Then learning everything about you to torture you inside jail or out.

They use ex-cons to mess with you and jail house mentality. One guy told me he had to hit a guy in jail first so he wouldn't be the bitch.

When I was in my element I was happy go lucky. I never thought much on killing, seven years later I'll kill anyone.

Why you may always get the same result is because some humans are violent assholes and don't understand sexuality, and may attack anything that is different or threatening to their own genetic makeup.

One thing leads to another and another and before you know it's mass hysteria. It may be true that my champain may have rewrote something on sexuality, we will see. Yes, it's important to get the bad guy, but don't think that some of these people in States or even in the State Department aren't sadistic narcissist.

This is why at some point the State has to come out of the dark. A bunch of people in different groups fighting over one person. The State really can't do its job. Inevitably Create some kind of dialogue and reconstruction. Even a protected status. Otherwise the individual may not delineate between the State and rogue individuals. Domestic terrorism.

You could literally hand someone the book and still get all the answers you need. T.J.W.

CHAPTER 3

Charts: 1. Thirty Plus Year Transformation & 2. Path

High School Maturity is not Dementia. T.J.W.

It is my belief that Magical thinking is not that deep. Personality Character and DNA is deep. I get magical thinking from being prompted by others. A transfer of information deep in the Kensho. I can not know everything they know. And they cannot see what I see. But it is like someone passing a flashlight of information to me. They will only know what I know when I bring it back to them.

What people are trying to understand at least partially may be in these two charts. In the Thirty Year Transformation chart there is elements I consider before and after a natural transformation. Some elements may exist or not exist for different people. I put what I think they are trying to see from my perspective.

A POST: "PJP is my soulmate. We share a reciprica; diversity. You have seen my line it is not your line for sure, but is the line that you should be looking at. Fantasy, dominance, jealousy and love. Marks the end of the dark years and primary maturity. I have seen her inner child more than once and it is the most beautiful thing you'll ever see. That tells me she was comfortable with me. And with her that's a rarity. When you start torturing diverse females to death people will start understanding what you're really doing." 4/06/21 tjw.

A POST:

"What a 30+ year Transformation does is allows my field to open wider. Is not a breakthrough although there are breakthroughs, it is a transformation. Although the outcome may not change a person's partners they might be considered to be a professional in sex, and sexuality at this point If not human behavior.

The primary difference between breaking a neck and kissing

a neck. Magical thinking probably doesn't occur in the early years. Being picked up by an intelligent 16 year old and dating for a few years is probably as normal as it gets. What do high school students really say about sex and dating.

If somebody with minimal violence or no violence makes it through their transformation in my estimate there is even less chance for violence or no violence following the transformation.

Kensho is the exception. And while deviant sex and "sexual crash" may exist following transformation I do not consider that to be violent.

As for individuals with violence pre transformation I can only go by data. If transformation would even be possible for those individuals I'm not sure.

Post transformation might look like more balanced relationships, a shift in social circles perhaps more even demeanor. Something geographical.

Although these differences may be very subtle.

I would not overlay the dark years and primary maturity as the same thing.

Primarily due to the chemicals and changes in the body,

what I call musk. I think maturity can continue after 27 years old for many males and females.

Anyone who has gone through a 30 plus year transformation Kensho's only value may be to make sure someone is awake or create violence". tjw.

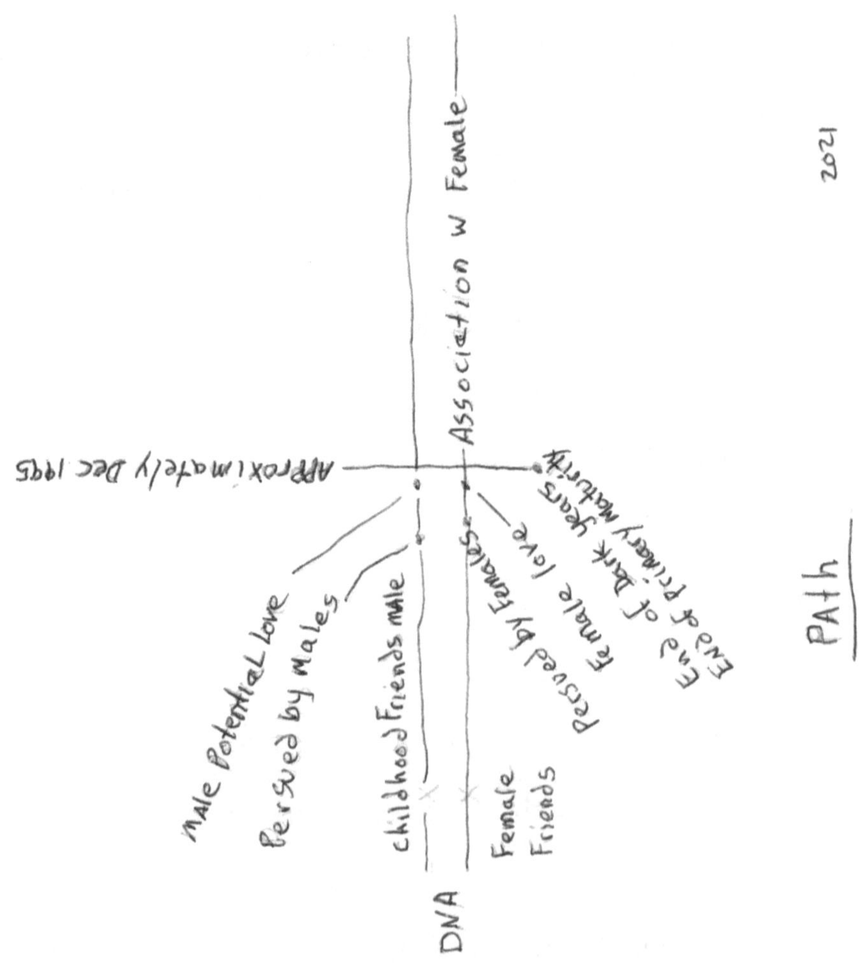

What the transformation did for me was open up the field. The Kensho besides make me a killer moved me to the feminine side. I usually like hanging out with the women anyway.

The PATH chart shows my sexual path. For both sexes. Not exactly the same as Neural Pathes but similar. Also this could be different for other people. But I would say a transformation is more likely to occur for many humans regardless of the outcome. Something I might call post transformation; navigating vs practicing or navigating vs non-practicing.

The divergence between the lines is what I call a true cognitive disobedience. Where both are valid, but may pit man against self or women against self. At least until it doesn't.

Interactions with both male and female as kid, non-sexual but emotional. (Outside of normal interactions with male and female as kid). So that a connection is noticed with both sexes.

Dark years and maturity does not seem to be an exact overlap. Maturity more with growth and dark years more with hormones and chemicals.

Association with female and sexual drive for female is primary.

Kensho seems to be able to destroy either or both paths. I

don't think your issue is that deep. If someone is deeply disturbed than that may be the case. However, it seems that most people just don't like sexually open people or are fearful of deviant sex.

I look at those charts as if there are three or four similar models for different people in a tight data group.

I do believe that searching does divide fear and age among other data, Sniffing the tail, pain, fear, abuse. I think that it is a natural condition. I have always been sexually driven as far back as I can remember. There should be a natural division if you look for it.

If it doesn't take long for people to screw up invite them to a class.

It's not necessarily uncontrolled choices. A lot closer to level of play, what someone would or would not do in life. This highlights a fundamental difference in types of people. A degree or level. Not dementia. Not violence. Sexually exploring open, play is highly intelligent. This is what I would align with the article on drinking and IQ.

Non violent
Sexually not open, not-
-NAVIgating.
Diverse, Non Diverse.
Dementia/magical Thinking

Non violent
Sexually open
Navigating
Sexually Diverse
Dementia/magical thinking

violent
Sexually not open not-
NAVigating. Diverse
Non Diverse
Dimentia/magical Thinking

violent
Sexually open
NAVigating
Diverse
Dimentia/magical thinking

NAVigational sexual quad   2021   NW.

While I don't have a memory and confirmation for every point on the chart I have enough to extrapolate a potential.

This chart should cover most anybody. While some elements in each quarter may or may not apply to a single person, it's primary purpose is to more closely understand a character type Specifically in relation to sexuality navigation and violence or not.

There could be more than one character type in each quadrant. Dementia or magical thinking if applicable might also relate to non-sexual thought process.

Some elements are not on the chart primarily because They

can be deceptive and biased and require deeper clarification. Or simple research.

Like lying, drugs and alcohol, outbursts. Also I would not put people under this filter for perfectionism that's a continued recipe for disaster.

I do not consider mutual consensual sex as violence, deviant or not.

*   *   *

I could put a perfect mom in the first quadrant non-violent non navigating. But says things that Sometimes just don't add up. Or just not plausible.

Or I could put a professional guy straight non navigating in the same quadrant who likes to get too close to boys. Nonviolent.

Theoretically I could put a physical plant worker in the third quadrant violent as hell. Straight non-diverse abused as a kid. Doesn't know why the sexuality he supposed to be comes up psychotic and violent every time it hits his consciousness.

The fourth quadrant may be the most rare for number of problems. Simply because people are sexually open navigating

which I consider to be an honest expression of human. However I could imagine a woman or man in conflict whom may actually be practicing both sexual sides but for some reason remains conflicted.

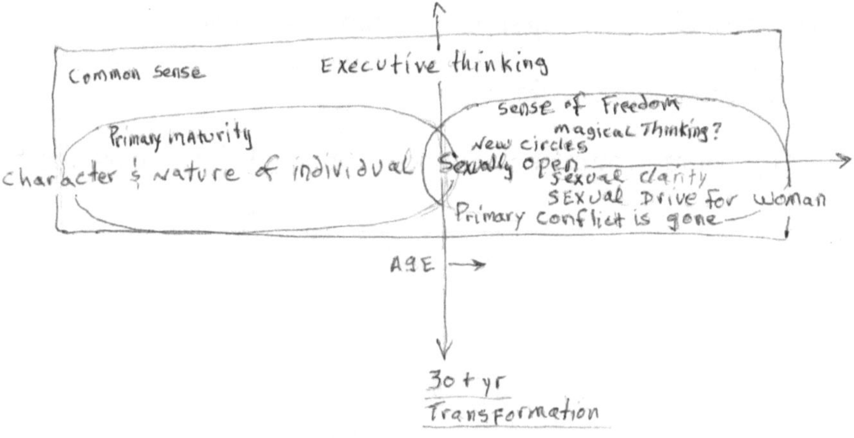

I know there was an incident in town so I can't blame you for Northfield if you did.

The circles probably don't line up anyway which probably you figured out. just back into town met her for the first time.

You see of a relationship like that There's not enough jealousy in a relationship for primarily two reasons. Number one is there's not enough time in on the relationship, and number two There's not enough vicarious mannerisms behaviors in the female to be jealous of. But this could vary.

Although jealousy played a part I think Primarily was a traditional relationship.

My theory on the incident is that you came across the right information but had a gap or roadblock somehow.

It's probably a classic case.

Any years around college our potential dark years for the male.

CHAPTER 4

The Political Path

If information comes from outside the state as non-violent, and then is acted on in a destructive manor, states may decide to withhold information in the future. Because if nothing else people go back and dig up anything they can for non-constructive purpose.

By 2005 I believe people were already starting to block me. Age 45. For something I had no idea of.

Work at the phone company was essentially just a waste of time. Just before that after several attempts someone attacked me with one black and white grainy picture. Opening up the State.

As I figured that some information was leaked to the company before my arrival. Not only about my previous girlfriend but that attack on my pc. I saw people quit over what they were doing to me.

Same waste of time for the next ten years.

They followed me to Argentina on vacation and back. And when things were getting hot I was going to leave the US. Interestingly, strangely, a girlfriend in Canada and one in Argentina both got in car accidents at the same time. One went to the hospital, one is dead.

At this point I had already been going to the alternative clubs for over ten years. Not sure if they forgot or not. Economy may change patterns.

Creating an execution committee behind closed doors and hiding it from the public is exactly what America stands against and goes to war over in third world countries.

Chapter 5

What Transformation Looks Like

If you ever come across a man having fits with himself, this may be pre transformation. After the thirty-year transformation there may be a sense of peace. Relationships should be more even or balanced. Although the outcome may not dictate who the individual will be with. I always moved a lot but something geographical probably. It's personal, so communication is probably filtered or protected.

If someone makes it through a thirty-year transformation there most likely will be a sense of peace for a while. Excluding Kensho, Economy and spouses.

The reality may be there are still many factors in finding a partner. Someone like Dr David Buss in Austin may be able to shed some light on this.

Chapter 6

The Argument

I think sex drive comes in more than one possibility. And that this is for the benefit of a stronger regenesis.

I'm not sure what exactly I may have changed but I know why. I decided to stand up for what I believe sexually. Even in the face of death. Most people may not even make it this far, let alone be able to write. So I think in that space people were able to see some things previously unclarified.

Also I think people realized that dating a sixteen-year-old thirty-five years ago is not the same thing as having sex with a baby.

It doesn't matter what you call it if people are getting massacred the fallout is pretty bad.

Twenty percent are being forced to change sexual orientation? I would say the results are mixed for many reason.

CHAPTER 7

Teaching Lessons

A post: One of Many truths.

I don't think anybody over there is in a place to tell me much about manipulation.

That's what seem to confuse people the most who follow my history. It's probably one of the most difficult elements to understand. Given my feedback.

I think they don't understand someone coming from a place of purity following their nature. Non narcissistic. Not perfect but someone who is inspired and driven.

A conscience relationship in understanding the full set of DNA and what it looks like. Instead I believe they think that it is a manipulation or untrue.

In fact, I consider someone who is sexually open to be the most true form of human. And an honest expression. where others pretend they are not.

A post: It's not really learning a lesson at thirty. It's an understanding. So if I believe both sexual attraction exists, two Paths, for me it's an evolution of my understanding that they even exist, and of what they really mean.

The thirty plus year transformation I believe takes care of the primary conflict. Although some questions may still remain.

I think researching someone life and teaching lessons with violence is violence. I don't think that lessons line up with source anyway. Taking half a story and creating a violent punishment seems a little mental to me. People in power are just as bias and racist. Isn't the idea to prevent violence. This is more than mission creep.

Chapter 8

Sniffing The Tail

I would say we are still creatures. Audio visual is still my primary communication. Visually connecting with people is normal. Searching checking is a natural part of humans I believe. People probably don't like that. There should be a natural division, fear and pleasure among other elements. I also would say that sexually open people could see kids grow up with no "Magical thinking" or sexual attachment.

I believe that sexual reciprocal starts at the chemical level. So that normal interaction creates interest in both parties for attraction. Creates chemical changes in the other.

Chapter 9

Bias

The Bias is unbelievable, yes it's important to be vigilant but clearly there are problems everywhere.

For starters scary to say almost no one on the opposition team would be in camp I would hang out with. Admittedly I'm a strange bird anyway. However, I noticed a very high percent of the group that followed servailed, influenced, harassed, blocked, attacked and threatened me were not people I would normally hang out with anyway.

Not that they shouldn't be protecting people but the fact is bias remains. The other condition I noticed was as my life was being deprived all sorts of other bias came into play. As I became pushed into the system and became beat down people just expected that I take certain drugs, or saw therapists. Which is all fine except that this wasn't on my mind at all and was startling to me.

Later my feedback was implying that I was connected to some murders that had taken place. There seemed to me to be a few insesive conditions that were repeatedly being beat into my presence. As if I was supposed to accept something as fact that was happenstance at best. Trying to fit or force a wrong piece of the jigsaw puzzle. This was highly disturbing and seemed bias to me.

And so over all bias is the norm to start from.

CHAPTER 10

The Reason Why People Don't Have Human Rights

As soon as the violence starts I loose simple access to things simply by fear or being blocked. No money no access. As soon as the state cracks that door they take on every little thing in the individual's life. Including health care.

Now fast forward someone seven years in that condition. I had to get water from the down spout from my old house to drink. One of my trips to the emergency room I couldn't even give a blood sample. They couldn't draw any blood I was so dehydrated. Not to mention I literally hyperventilated for five years.

If you're in a world that suddenly you may have to kill or be killed any second year after year you will lose your rights too. Setting someone up in this context is an execution.

CHAPTER 11

Hijacking An Erection

Not sure exactly due to the time past and violence but I would say this occurs over several months for most people into a campaign. The phenomenon is very real. And one of the scariest events in my life. Crossed wires are real, "mesh" and probably some have been tortured to death in the most horrific way due to this test/phenomenon.

It's based in fear in connection with implying a desire for children. Two years give or take from the onset of violence. Once the concept of conspiracy was known the fear goes to work.

Attacking someone with child pornography and then violence and then throwing babies in their face implying desire creates a path in my head from -that's not what I want-then visualizing what I do want, creating a loop based in fear. Probably from a place of judgement. Given the insanity and violence that is currently going on around me this only makes sense. So now the fear is attached to the loop connected to the thought process of arousal.

The loop is burned over and over into the brain until everything in that loop moves the needle. Fear is the common denominator so that fear works even connected to other conditions called up. The fear that I'm talking about is not tripping over my shoe lace, it's any fear that is connected to the arena of sex and accusation. Although there is some random fear that I noticed is seemingly connected.

"Mesh" crossed wires seems to occur on the back side of all of that. Perhaps that's when it becomes noticeable. Its deep and dark. The phenomenon does drop off after a few years incrementally, but the memory of process still remains.

Chapter 12

Health

The initial process of Kensho, fear starts at anger, moves into rage and off the chart past murder. Rage is new one for me, not very nice. But once into murder a second time the place starts to look familiar.

This is possible because of frustration and loss. The kind I would say most people don't really experience in life. It's an ongoing loss and insult that is starting the killing process. A focused attack that is understood that is forcing such great lose that its beyond logical.

Once Murder or off the chart is experienced a couple of times it became safer to exist in that state. A place of security, hence a killer is made. Laws and rules evaporate.

The stress and initial fear creates a chemical cocktail in

the body. A water mark and imprint on the micro level. The caritin in my nails changed color. And based on the growth it was approximately a three-month process of early stage of the champain.

The stress knocked out my pancreas and my body went into a diabetic state. Also The fluids and chemical output is out. Wax dries up in my ears, the fibers in my body tear easily, and it's like having concrete in my total system. My tear ducts visibly scarred over, at one point for several months I stopped dreaming. Just black. Maybe a pseudo form of sleep for about a year.

My eyesight may have been effected, not sure. Possibly a small heart attack and two small strokes.

The ongoing stress effects my brain on an increasing level. To the point of nerve damage. Acute pain in total body and twitching shaking. Lose of focus and train of thought. General mental erosion.

Two neural path loops were closed. this is probably a specific element per person. Most likely long term stress of fear for a specific condition. Maybe three to nine months under stress of a fear may close a thought process. When it happens it will be

Instantaneous, autonomous, and as far as I know irreversible. Perhaps new paths can be made under the right conditions?

The general wear and tear, pain and stress on the body becomes non tolerant.

CHAPTER 13

My Key Elements

- I think the brain categorizes some extremes by emotional poles. From pain to pleasure. And the two groups are primarily divided by emotion of those extremes. Perhaps in some cases, with little or no other path to some elements in those categories. I would guess that this may not be well understood by many humans. More of an epiphany and pretty deep into the conscience or sub conscience. So one emotional pole could contain anything with context of pain or fear. The other elements of pleasure or euphoria.

- Lying or not doesn't necessarily get any good information, sexually open is an honest expression.

- I have seen Thirty plus year transformations in both men and women as well as in myself.

- Why they don't necessarily mean same sex relationship is for many reasons, like no current match. Got run over by the State. Economic downturn. Change in sentiment or path due to experiences, understandings, any number of factors.

- Thirty plus year transformations should reduce violence if any, post transformation.

- Searching should have a division of "Sniffing the tail" nonviolent, and sexual pairing nonviolent. So that there should be a natural division in sexual and non-sexual. A normal chemistry should occur over a day or two if not years.

- Forcing someone into a sexual orientation may not be safer than home.

- After the abuse my kid and my family went through nobody can say this is for the kids. That's bullshit! It's a white racist beast assault. People need to be looking at individuals in government to law enforcement to local organized individuals.

- Once someone has acknowledged a second sexual path and there is an understanding of such, there should be a stand down policy with benefits. I've been going to alternative clubs for many years if someone goes for two days that would tell me intent.

- Move the law to the middle so everybody is unhappy. That ensures that its equally placed. If people are being slaughtered for dating than you should change the name from statutory rape to murder. Or change the law. At least it will reflect the truth. Don't even put an age on it. It becomes a target. Make it a simple process.

- Information or attachment as object of desire.

Last Chapter

What they did was, track me for years, unknown to me, then in the last almost two decades start blocking my efforts at work and financial and business and communications with immediate family.

This included having my wife brake down then block my call from her leaving her stranded. And very upset. This went on several times over the years dividing us. why she could not get any help from me when she needed it most. Why the calls never went through over and over again.

They would use this strategy in many ways. Even in the home, Neighborhood and around town. Dividing and frustrating our family anyway they could. Including and still to this day hypnosis on my daughter against me.

They would look for ways to block payments in the commercial level, create fraud on debit cards and block insurance payments. Stop buisness ventures and investments.

At this point Im probably running through the great recession three jobs trying to save two houses. In one of the worst counties in the country for foreclosures I was glad I argued for a fixed rate. Still working too hard. And ended up lost a lot but still had great credit a house and a little to start back with, and a new job. only to have them take that and everything else including my health.

*   *   *

They surveilled the house. Came in when I was at work with or without a permit, I don't think they care. Took and did whatever they wanted multiple times.

After several years of being blocked from work with multiple months off I was heading into work on a bicycle.

First day going back to work and was knocked clear across one lane of oncoming traffic.

I had to literally pull tmy bicycle out from under the truck wheel as he backed up.

Lucky to be alive left bloody I bent the wheel back on my bike and went to work.

With threat of jail for non-payment and the threat of being tortured in jail I had to go to work but I couldn't afford bankruptcy at this time.

A few days later oddly enough, the construction site supervisor let me go.

Have had the water at work poisoned they get my supervisor to give to me. Put flesh eating bacteria on my handlebars. And multiple violent on road incidents.

And once they scare you and use fear to get you to prove your orientation or sexual interest they will block your dating or sexual attempts until they set you up with somebody with HIV, try to prove you incompetent or just waste your time.

Don't do anything except for what you need to do to survive. Get a gun.

They poisoned the dog multiple times, probably people in the family as well. Poisoned me multiple times. Including have my boss hand me a plate of food that sent me to the hospital, and burned my insides.

Primarily because I was a target, for being sexually open. Someone new my history that wasn't even in my mind. Then being set up multiple times including pornography. At this point I now am carrying a semi-automatic hand gun. And expect to kill or be killed.

Whatever information they can get from family, friends, or organizations they try to use it against me. Or turn around half the story. Found that rather interesting.

Changing electronics in the house, hacking and destroying devices laptops, Threatening emails. Setting up software on my devices and local electronic parameter. Conning people to help destroy someone. Probably unknown to most of them Year after year.

Now homeless, pushed off the emotional chart and in bad health.

Blocking someone access to their second sexual side is something that will most likely bring on a highly charged reaction. Like communicating with an alternative club to lock someone out. If they come back with an AK-47 and slaughter the club how many times do you need to know that lesson ...

While people sit back and smirk.

www.ingramcontent.com/pod-product-compliance
Lightning Source LLC
Chambersburg PA
CBHW051419250726

48655CB00003B/1127